WHAT'S YOUR SPORT? CRICKET

WHAT'S YOUR SPORT?
CRICKET

CHRIS COWDREY
WITH DAVID LEMMON

PARTRIDGE PRESS

LONDON · NEW YORK · TORONTO · SYDNEY · AUCKLAND

TRANSWORLD
PUBLISHERS LTD
61-63 Uxbridge Road,
London W5 5SA

TRANSWORLD
PUBLISHERS
(AUSTRALIA) PTY LTD
15-23 Helles Avenue,
Moorebank NSW 2170

TRANSWORLD
PUBLISHERS (NZ) LTD
Cnr Moselle and
Waipareira Aves,
Henderson, Auckland

Published 1989 by
Partridge Press
a division of Transworld
Publishers Ltd
Copyright © Christopher
Cowdrey 1989

British Library
Cataloguing in
Publication Data
Cowdrey, Christopher
    Cricket. – (What's your
    sport)
    1. Cricket
    I. Title   II. Lemmon,
    David
    796.35'8

ISBN 1–85225–063–1

Printed in Great Britain
by Mackays of Chatham
PLC,
Letchworth

Design Graham Mitchener
Illustrations Chris Lyon
All photographs by
Patrick Eagar except for:
11, 28 by S & G

CONTENTS

INTRODUCTION
BY CHRIS COWDREY

In the eyes of many, I had a privileged entry into the game of cricket. My father played more than one hundred times for England and was captain of both his county and his county, so I was taught and encouraged from an early age. I went to a preparatory school in Broadstairs and played in the school team at the age of nine.

At the age of thirteen I moved on to Tonbridge School. The wickets were good, the facilities excellent, the coaching first rate. At the age of fourteen I played in the Tonbridge first eleven for the first time. Later to be with me in the Tonbridge side were Richard Ellison, now my colleague at Kent, and Nick Kemp, who also played for Kent for a while before moving on to Middlesex.

When I was sixteen I played for Young England at Lord's, and two years later I was captain of the Young England side that went to the West Indies. David Gower, Mike Gatting, Ian Gould, Bill Athey, Paul Allott and Paul Downton were all in the party.

I won a place in the Kent side, and in 1979 I was awarded my country cap – the badge of recognition of having made the grade.

I played five times for England in India in 1984–5 with David Gower's side, and the following summer I became captain of Kent. I have led my county in a Lord's final and known the disappointment of being on the losing side, however narrowly.

Setting the record down like this may give the impression that it has all been an easy and quite logical progression, and that I can have no understanding of or feeling for the young player, or older player, who is keen to play at the most humble level. That is not the case.

The fact that I had a father who was one of the most eminent figures in the game was not always an advantage. However helpful he was to me personally, there were always those who wished to judge me by his standards. This was inevitable, but it was also very unfair. We were totally different in our approaches to the game.

The fact that I had a father who was one of the most eminent figures in the game was *not* always an advantage

My eagerness to play my shots has tended to make my father look upon me as a little impetuous at times. Most of his career was played when there was less emphasis on limited-over cricket, and, in fact, in spite of his 114 Tests, he played in only one one-day international, the first. In addition, the comparisons with my father have made it rather harder for me to assert my own individual style.

I am conscious, too, that I have had several friends who would like to have played first-class cricket and were denied the opportunity, and that many of my friends and colleagues in Kent and other counties have had very different starts in the game from my own.

Simon Hinks played for Kent Schools. Steve Marsh came to be Alan Knott's successor through his performances in club cricket. Trevor Ward found his way to Kent after going to school in Wales. None of them had the advantage of enjoying the same facilities that my brother Graham, Richard Ellison, Chris Tavaré and I enjoyed when we were younger, but they have all fought their way into first-class cricket.

If this book uses the examples of first-class cricketers, it is because they are easy to understand and accessible to all. To mention Ian Botham or David Gower is to give the reader an instantly recognisable picture. But this book is not about first-class cricket, and only a handful of those who read it are ever likely to follow cricket as a profession. It is a book for those who have a passion for the game, who are eager to play it, who want to know more about it, and who want to know where they should go for help and advice.

To have a love of cricket and a desire to play it can be both frustrating and depressing if you do not know whom to approach or where to start. Clubs, kit, laws, style, averages, sizes of bats – a host of things can be thrust at you which will leave you only lonely and bewildered. This is an attempt to tell you to whom you should turn and what help you can expect, and even how much it is likely to cost you.

I would suggest that more friendships have been brought about by cricket than by any other game. It is by its very nature social, and it can stand you well wherever you go in the world. If you should find yourself suddenly working in Denmark, Canada, Holland, Papua New Guinea, Singapore, Bermuda or Hong Kong, you can be sure that, if you can play a bit of cricket, there are clubs you can join and friends who will welcome you. Cricket is a passport to companionship and, if only for that reason, it should be cherished and enjoyed.

One final point concerns the advice given about buying equipment, books etc. To make the information as useful as possible actual prices are given. These all refer to the situation in late 1988, when the book was written; prices do change!

1 GETTING STARTED

In the opinion of most followers of cricket, the greatest batsman who has ever lived is the Australian Don Bradman. When he was three years old Bradman's family moved to a town called Bowral, eighty miles from the large city of Sydney, with transport far more difficult than it is today. Living in a remote area, his friends many miles away, Bradman found, as a boy, that he had to play games like cricket and football on his own. Cricket was his passion, and he devised a game which he could play and practise on his own, using a golf ball, an old stump and a brick wall. The stump was used as a bat; he threw the ball against the wall and attempted to hit it as it came back, generally very quickly. At other times he would throw the ball or bowl the ball against the wall and field or catch the return.

However useful and single-minded Bradman's early cricket self-education was, it had no meaning until he began to play in his school and local teams. Cricket is a team game, and can be fully enjoyed only when one is part of a team, working with ten others.

The essential worth of cricket is to achieve what is good for the team To do well – to take ten wickets or score a hundred runs – is the delight and the aim of all, but the essential worth of cricket is to achieve what is good for the team at any particular time. That may mean scoring a quick ten or twenty rather than a slow fifty or hundred. It may mean staying in, defending fiercely so that you

do not lose your wicket, while somebody else gets the run. It could mean bowling defensively in order to frustrate the batsmen so that other bowlers reap the harvest and take the wickets. It may even mean making the vital stop which turns a four into a single.

Bernard Hollowood, who played club and village cricket all over England, recalled an incident many years ago when he was batting so slowly in a Staffordshire League match that his own captain wanted him out.

After an hour and a half at the crease I had made only thirty. There were signals from the pavilion, and of course I understood them. Yet try as I would I could not let the bat go. I charged up the wicket to ball after ball, but I found myself miserably incapable of following through when applying the bat to the most tempting of half-volleys.

A wicket fell and the new batsman hurried in. He tapped the first ball to cover, called me for a run, and then stood his ground, smiling, while cover-point lobbed the ball to the bowler and ran me out by about eighteen yards. Afterwards, when the winning runs had been made, the batsman bought me a drink. 'Sorry about that, Bernard,' he said, 'but it had to be done. Skipper's orders.'

Bernard Hollowood was born into a cricketing family, and it was quite natural for him, when in his early teens, to join the practice at Burslem Cricket Club and to become a member of the club. Not everyone today has so straightforward a path into the game, but the paths are still there and the doors at the end are opened by people who are very willing to help in every way.

There are very few towns or villages in England that do not have a cricket club of some standard within easy reach. In large cities the problem is more difficult, but sports centres have evolved which give assistance in all sports and where the warden will direct young people, and older people, towards clubs and institutions which foster the growth and health of cricket. In Haringey in north London, for example, there is a cricket school which has provided coaching and facilities for hundreds of young people and has helped to find them clubs where they can prosper and enjoy their cricket. The Gloucestershire all-rounder Mark Alleyne, who has played for Young England, is a product of this school.

THE NATIONAL CRICKET ASSOCIATION

For a variety of reasons ranging from time and facilities available to inadequate provision of supervision, many young people have had little experience of playing cricket as part of a team at school. With their lack of such experience, they may feel daunted and nervous about approaching a club, particularly if it has an imposing ground and superb facilities. In these cases, as in much else, the National Cricket Association is there to help.

The National Cricket Association was set up in 1965 with the object of aiding and encouraging all recreational cricket, that is all cricket which is not first-class county cricket. It organises coaching on a national level, distributes the money that comes from government sources and from charities so that it benefits local cricketers, assists in ground maintenance and in the promotion of artificial wickets, and offers advice and help in every area. The NCA works through its fifty county organisations so that once again there is a local institution to which the young cricketer can turn, but the NCA itself will advise anyone and put them in touch with a club near to where they live or with their county association.

The National Cricket Association is centred with the Test and County Cricket Board at Lord's, and the address is:

The Secretary
National Cricket Association
Lord's Cricket Ground
St John's Wood
London NW8 8QN

Another, more recent organisation is the Arundel Castle Cricket Foundation in Sussex. This is a charitable organisation set up to help young cricketers, particularly those at school, by providing coaching and training in the lovely grounds of Arundel Castle where there is a fine new indoor cricket school. The centre is run by John Barclay, the former Sussex captain, and although it is primarily intended to help groups of cricketers from schools and city sports centres, it will offer advice and assistance to all. Although situated in Sussex, the Foundation aims to spread its work to all parts of the country. John Barclay is rich in experience of the game and the most helpful of men. For information, write to:

J. R. T. Barclay
Arundel Castle Cricket Foundation
Arundel Park
Sussex BN18 9LH

Eventually, however, contact must be made with the club itself, for that is where the cricket is played.

CRICKET CLUBS

Cricket clubs throughout England are conscious of the needs of young people and of the lack of provision that exists in some schools, and many have taken on the responsibility of providing the coaching and junior matches which were once the province of schools. All cricket clubs are willing to help and encourage young players because they look to them for their futures. Some will come to them coached and proficient, having played organized cricket for four or five years; others will have nothing but their enthusiasm to commend them – that is sufficient.

Initial contact is usually made with the secretary of a club, for he will know who is most appropriate in the club to deal with a new recruit and will be able to advise what is available.

One joins a club because one wants to play cricket, but as a young player patience is needed. A club will be assessing new members for what they can bring to a team, not just on the playing side, but in their commitment to the social and administrative side of the club. A club can exist only because people are willing to do such jobs as sweep the pavilion, put up and take down nets, set out boundary pegs, move sight-screens, sell raffle tickets and even mow the pitch. In many cases, without these things a club would be able to provide no cricket, and only by entering fully into the life of a club does a member derive the full benefit from all that the game entails.

Each step up the ladder that one takes in cricket, as in all aspects of life, is a challenge. The good cricketer at school will invariably open both the batting and the bowling and be the captain. If he is chosen for a district side, he will find himself in the company of ten others at least six of whom, one would wager, are also opening batsmen, opening bowlers and captains. He has to adjust accordingly.

The move to club cricket presents a further challenge, for the standard will be higher, the players more thoughtful, technically sounder and richer in experience with a wider knowledge of the game. A young player should listen and learn.

The desire to bat and bowl most of the time is strong in all of us, but what is good for the progress of the team and the individual is what is **In whatever team you play, you can** of paramount importance. A young **always prove yourself to your teamates** cricketer new to the club may feel **by your attitude in the field** that he should be playing in a team above the one for which he has been selected, but the club may feel, rightly, that he has a better chance of development batting at number four or five in the second team and bowling a few overs rather than batting eight or nine in the first eleven, rarely getting to the wicket and never bowling at all. In whatever team you play, you can always prove yourself by your attitude in the field.

Graham Gooch was in Ilford second eleven when he was first invited to play for Essex; he was opening for Ilford, but when he played for Essex in a Sunday league game he batted number nine and did not bowl. Professional cricketers, too, have to make their

adjustments, come to terms with the higher standard in which they are playing.

Ole Mortensen, the best cricketer to emerge from Denmark, has batted at number four for his club and his country and has been a prolific scorer. At Derbyshire, he has never batted higher than number ten. John Lever of Essex, Paul Jarvis of Yorkshire and Neal Radford of Worcestershire are others who have scored many runs at club level but bat in the lower order in the county side.

Starting at a new club or with a new team implies starting at the bottom, and great cricketers such as Denis Compton, one of the most exciting batsmen the game has known, and Ian Botham, for several years the leading all-rounder in the world, began on the ground staff at Lord's where they swept the terraces after big matches and sold scorecards in between playing their junior matches and receiving instruction. At cricket one is learning all the time, by direct coaching, by talking, by listening, by discussing, by reading and by watching. The process never ends.

John Childs was twenty-four years old before Gloucestershire noticed him playing in Devon and offered him a contract. He played for them for nine years with considerable success until it was felt that his slow left-arm bowling no longer had the potency that it once had. Childs accepted the fact that his first-class cricket career was over and prepared to return to his business as a sign-writer. To his surprise, Essex, at the time the leading side in the country, approached him to join them, and he gladly accepted the opportunity.

His first year with Essex was one of misery and disaster. He took only five wickets for very many runs, so confirming Gloucestershire's lack of faith, but there were those at Essex who still believed that his lapse in form and confidence need be only temporary. He spent a winter working with, and talking to, Fred Titmus, the great Middlesex spin bowler and Test selector. The following year, his self-belief restored by hard work and careful thought, he was the leading spin bowler in England and played a vital

Opposite:
Graham Gooch, a massive striker of the ball, but a batsman who can shape his game to fit the needs of his side.

17

part in Essex winning the County Championship.

Childs came later to cricket than most. His county colleague Paul Prichard was coached at Hutton Cricket Club when he was eight and played for Essex Schools when he was nine. There is no set pattern for entering club cricket or first-class cricket. It is never too early, and it is never too late.

Dennis Amiss, whose batting was a delight to watch because he was technically so accomplished, was noticed playing in a schools cricket match when he was sixteen and immediately offered a contract by Warwickshire. Eighty years ago, one of England's great batsmen, 'Patsy' Hendren, was seen playing cricket in the street against a lamp post. He was taken to Turnham Green Cricket Club at the age of eleven and five years later was with Middlesex. Jack Simmons came to Lancashire from League cricket at the age of twenty-seven; Mike Gatting came to Middlesex straight from school.

In club cricket one has known players come up in the traditional manner from the colts' side, while others, found standing at a bus stop, have been asked if they would like a game because the side was one short.

Perhaps the most romantic story of all concerning a person's start in first-class cricket is that relating to Harold Gimblett. He was playing village cricket in Somerset, and it was suggested that he should go for a county trial. He was watched batting in the nets, but he impressed nobody; he was told not to bother to come again. Then it was discovered that Somerset were a man short for the match at Frome against Essex. The only player whom they could contact was Gimblett. He was told to be at Bridgwater at nine o'clock, from where he would be given a lift. This meant getting up at five in the morning, which he did, but he still missed the bus. As he walked along the country lanes, a lorry picked him up and took him to Bridgwater. Somerset batted first, and he was put at number eight although he had come for his trial as an opening batsman. When he went in the county were

in trouble. He hit 123. His hundred was the fastest of the season – 63 minutes – and won him the Lawrence Trophy. The following season he was in the England side as an opener.

Most club and village cricketers do not become first-class players, but energy, enthusiasm, applica-**A continual willingness to learn will** tion and a continual willingness to learn **always help a cricketer to improve** will always help a cricketer to improve, in order to reach his best possible standard.

As indicated earlier, in large cities where the nearest cricket club may not be easily accessible, there are sports centres which provide facilities for cricket practice and much else. Sometimes these sports centres are new and impressive buildings; sometimes they are converted warehouses or factories; very often they are on school premises and serve the dual purpose of catering for the school in the day-time and for the general public in the evening. Always they will be of help to the aspiring cricketer.

As well as offering nets in which to practise, and sometimes technical advice, many sports centres also give the opportunity to play indoor cricket. This is a comparatively new and highly popular game which, while following all the basic laws and techniques of cricket, requires fewer people and less equipment. The warden of the local sports centre will be able to give information and introductions.

The consistent factor, whether you go to a cricket club, a cricket association, the Arundel Castle Trust, your local sports centre or any other sporting organisation linked to cricket, is that there will always be somebody who will help, advise and encourage. No problem is insurmountable.

Two stories relating to first-class cricketers will provide examples of what can be achieved with perseverance. Glenn Turner lived in New Zealand but wanted to play cricket in England so that he could improve his game and play professionally. To earn the money to pay his fare to England he worked every night for a year in a bakery. He came to England and applied to various counties. Warwickshire invited him to come and practise in the nets. They looked at him and said that although they could not offer him an engagement, they would introduce him to Worcestershire. By the end of his career he had become the finest batsman New Zealand had produced and was the scorer of more than a hundred hundreds.

Andy Moles was a club cricketer who wanted more than anything else to be a county cricketer. He wrote to all seventeen counties, but the only one to offer him encouragement was Warwickshire. Within a year he had forced his way into the Warwickshire first team, and within two years he had been awarded his county cap and was becoming one of the most reliable opening batsmen in the country.

2 EQUIPMENT

One thing that makes young people hesitate before taking up cricket as a recreation or makes an older person reluctant to return to the sport after a few years' absence is the belief that it is an expensive game. Many fear that they simply will not be able to afford the equipment that is necessary. Let us now look at the question of equipment and its cost.

The following items can all be considered part of a cricketer's equipment:

white shirt
white trousers
white sweater
bat
pads
batting gloves
boots or reinforced sports shoes (white)
protector
thigh pad
cap or sun hat
helmet

To the professional cricketer these are all essential items, but for the first-class player, cricket is his job of work; it is his means of earning a living. His equipment comprises the tools of his trade, and he is using it seven days a week. For the weekend cricketer and the beginner, the needs are different. His equipment should be comfortable, affordable and should provide suitable protection.

CLOTHING

Clothing is essential because it is personal. Every cricketer must possess his own shirts and trousers. The cost of a cricket shirt of reputable make (Duncan Fearnley, Gray Nicholls, Bukta etc.) will vary from £10 to £25, and generally there is a discount for young players who buy two shirts at a time. There is no need whatsoever to buy the most expensive. You need only buy what feels right for you and what you can afford, although one would suggest that often to buy very cheap equipment is a waste of money, for it will neither last nor serve you well.

The prices quoted above are for long-sleeved shirts. Short-sleeved shirts are fifty pence to a pound cheaper, but you should remember that the summer in England is not always encouraging for short sleeves.

A pair of cricket trousers, again by a reputable manufacturer, will cost anything from £10 to £35; here again the price depends upon the quality. Styles alter, and one should wear the style which feels most comfortable whether it is elasticated waist and tie cord or the older and more conventional zip fly and hook.

Footwear is a more expensive item than shirts or trousers. A pair of white training shoes or gym shoes comes cheaply and, in appearance, these will serve, but cricket is played with a hard ball which can hurt and damage if it hits you. The feet are vulnerable and should be protected, particularly when batting. For cricket boots or cricket shoes, one must choose a good manufacturer. The prices range from around £12.50 for lightweight, but re-enforced, shoes to £40 for boots. Choose boots or shoes with care: they are a most important part of any cricketer's equipment.

There is one other item of equipment which is indispensable and that is a protector or 'box'. Even if you are primarily a bowler or a wicket-keeper, you will have to bat. A box not only gives protection, it gives confidence. It is the first thing that a cricketer needs to buy.

There is no need to rush to the nearest sports shop to buy equipment. There is a variety of choice, and you will find that magazines such as *The Cricketer* and other publications carry several pages which amount to cricket equipment catalogues. They will point prospective buyers to the dealers who are able to make the best offers. An even better method of buying equipment is to order through a cricket or sports club, which invariably obtain good quality at discount prices. Again it is an area in which sound advice and help is always forthcoming.

BATS, PADS AND GLOVES

Another way in which a cricket club helps younger players is to carry a club bag for junior or lower teams. This will contain bats, pads and gloves which may be used by all, although obviously every cricketer should strive to collect his own equipment for his personal use – there is little joy in pulling on a pair of batting gloves which have just been worn by somebody else for an hour or so.

Batting gloves, like all other equipment, vary in quality and price, which ranges from below £10 to around £25. There are two considerations when choosing gloves: Do they offer adequate protection for the hands? do they feel comfortable when you hold a bat wearing them? It is these two factors which should determine your choice.

The last piece of protection is the thigh pad. It is possible to buy a thigh pad, but it is far easier, and cheaper, to make one. All that is needed is a material that will offer resistance to a cricket ball, such as foam or a piece of carpet underlay, and some ribbon to sew on to it so that it may be tied round the thigh. Again, make sure that it is comfortable to wear. Whatever job you are doing, whatever sport you are playing, you will do better if you feel comfortable and at ease while you are in action.

The thigh pad, of course, is worn on the leg which is thrust forward at the bowler. For the right-handed batsman, that is the left leg; for the left-handed batsman, it is the right leg. This is a simple case which everyone understands, but it must also be remembered

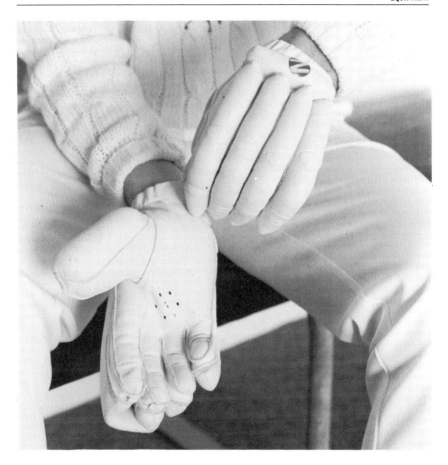

that when buying pads and gloves there is a difference between those manufactured for left-handed and right-handed batsmen, and you need to make sure that you are getting what is right for you.

It is possible to pay as much as £50 for a high-quality pair of batting pads, but it is certainly equally possible to buy a perfectly satisfactory pair of canvas pads for approximately £20. Another alternative in buying a pair of pads, or indeed in buying much other equipment, is to find a second-hand pair for half the normal price. Cricket clubs can often help in this direction, but the cricketing magazines and press frequently carry advertisements for stocks of cricketing equipment that, for a variety of reasons,

Equipment should be carefully chosen and looked after well. Chris Cowdrey pulls on his batting gloves.

is being sold or auctioned at much reduced prices. Nobody can tell you that this will happen regularly at certain places; it is an item of news for which you need to keep your eyes open.

Sweaters can be bought. You can pay anything up to £40 for a plain, long-sleeved sweater, but most clubs will have their own sweaters which are offered at reasonable prices and which carry the club colours. Alternatively, a sweater could provide a relative with an ideal opportunity to knit a present for Christmas or birthday!

The one item that has not yet been mentioned is that which is the first that most cricketers acquire – a bat. You can pay as much as a hundred pounds for a bat, or you can pay as little as seventeen, but generally bats are precious and expensive and should be chosen with care.

Bats are precious and expensive and should be chosen with care

There are two types of bat, the natural and the polyarmoured, and they need looking after in different ways. Bats vary in weight, but it is not the *dead* weight of a bat which should affect your choice, rather the pick-up weight which should tell you how well the bat is balanced to your liking. Bats generally have hard use in club cricket, and not always the best of treatment, so that one would normally advise against a bat which weighs less than 2 lb 6 oz, although again it is the balance and the pick-up weight which count.

A natural bat needs much care and attention before you play with it. Before using the bat treat it with a light film of linseed oil once a week for the first four weeks and thereafter once a month. You should oil the face, back, edges and toe of the bat, but not the splice. Do not over-oil the bat, for that will weaken it.

Having given your bat its first four weeks of oiling, you should begin to knock it in. If your club possesses a bat facing hammer (a wooden mallet specifically made for knocking in bats), use it to give the bat regular, gentle taps. Most probably, you will use an old leather ball to knock in the bat, tapping the ball gently up and down with the bat at regular intervals.

Opposite:
A bat is an expensive piece of equipment and needs care and attention.

Denis Compton. It is the man and not the tools that makes a cricketer.

From this advice, you will realise that the ideal time to buy a bat is at the end of one season so that you can get it ready for use by the beginning of the next. If you damage your bat in any way, stop using it. Take it back to the makers; they are always willing to replace, repair or advise.

A polyarmoured bat is ready for use. It should never be oiled, but it should be looked after. Wipe the blade with a clean rag after use, and keep the bat dry. If it is broken or damaged, take it out of use.

Most cricketers seem to worry more about their bats than they do about any other piece of equipment. They also tend to blame their bats for all their troubles and failings, hitting them on the ground when they play a bad shot or even throwing them down in dressing rooms when they have been got out. Both actions can harm a bat, and every time you curse a bat for your own weaknesses and technical deficiencies, remember Denis Compton.

Compton played for Middlesex and England, and for many people he was the most exciting batsman who ever played cricket. In 1947 he scored more runs and hit more centuries in a season than any other man before or since. He was notoriously forgetful and frequently had to borrow bats from his colleagues because he had not remembered to bring one of his own. Naturally, his friends became tired of this and hid their bats when they saw him coming. In 1954, playing for England against Pakistan at Trent Bridge, Nottingham, he was just about to go to the wicket when he realised that he had again forgotten his bat. His team-mates flatly refused to lend him one so he picked up an old practice bat that was standing in the corner of the dressing room. Less than five hours later he was out, having scored 278, the highest Test score ever made at Trent Bridge, with a bat that no one else would have considered using. It is the man, and not the tools, that makes a cricketer.

When one adds towels and washing materials, a cricketer has a considerable amount of equipment to take to a match. All the more reason for not making his load heavier with a bag which is too heavy to carry. In going to a match you have to climb on and off buses or trains or squeeze into a car with other players and their equipment, so whatever you pack your kit into, this must be a consideration.

One final point. It is very easy to run to the shops and buy a lot of equipment for which you can pay a great deal of money. It is more prudent to talk to an older club member or to the secretary who will guide, advise on quality and needs and even help to save money.

3 IN THE MEANTIME

The cricket season lasts for approximately five months, and not even a professional cricketer plays on every day of the season. One would never suggest that every minute of every day should be spent practising or learning about cricket, but much can be done in the winter months or on idle summer days to bring you closer to the game and to improve techniques.

It has already been told in the second section of this book how Don Bradman practised in his back garden and how that practice helped him to become one of the very greatest of batsmen, and there are many stories similar to Bradman's of boys playing on their own against brick walls or lamp-posts until they became proficient. But the winter months in England do not encourage anyone to spend too much time outside, so let us consider alternative methods of improving one's cricket.

The Golden Age of English cricket is generally reckoned to be the twenty years before the outbreak of the First World War in 1914. It was a time particularly noted for some great amateur players such as C.B. Fry and W.G. Grace who were outstanding in many sports. Fry was an athlete and a soccer player; Grace was a champion hurdler as well as the most famous of cricketers. Another great player of the time was Sir Stanley Jackson, who became a noted politician as well as an outstanding England all-rounder and captain and member of a champion Yorkshire side.

Jackson was talented in many directions. He served with distinction in the army, was chairman of the selectors who chose the England side in 1934, and was Governor-General of Bengal in India. Being able to give less and less time to cricket because of his other interests, he decided to take up golf. He had never played the game before, but he spent the whole of one winter practising strokes in front of a mirror and referring to text-books. He did not actually hit a ball, but when he went out on to the golf course the following summer he was able to hold his own with anybody and to beat golfers who had been playing for several years.

One uses the example of a cricketer turning golfer but the process could just as easily be reversed, although, as the ball is still waiting to **The constant striving to perfect** be hit in golf and it is projected at you **technique should be the aim of** in cricket, it is unlikely that success **every cricketer** would be as immediate. Yet the model is a good one. The constant striving to perfect technique should be the aim of every cricketer, and the first steps towards a correct technique are to ensure that stance, or delivery, is right and comfortable.

MIRROR PRACTICE

Let us first consider batting. By standing in front of a mirror, you can determine whether your stance is correct. The shoulder and the elbow should be round to face the bowler, yet you should never wrench yourself into a position that makes you uncomfortable. The hands should be close together at the top of the handle with the fingers and thumbs curled round the handle. The head should be up and the eyes level so that you are looking straight at the bowler (the mirror). The knees are slightly bent for comfort and the shoulders still so that the eyes are level and the view of the bowler and the ball is clear. The bat is lifted back *straight* over the off stump and comes down *straight*, so that you hit the ball with the full face of the bat. In playing a drive to the off, you should be able to look

The traditional batting stance.

The bowler's arm comes over. The bat is raised in readiness.

The follow through
of a fluent off-drive
by Chris Cowdrey.

straight along the blade of the bat as you follow through in the direction in which you have hit the ball. As you stand awaiting a delivery, you can either stand with bat just behind the toes of the back foot resting lightly on the ground or, as taller players have done in recent years, wait for the ball with the bat held off the ground. It is a matter of preference or comfort but, for younger and less experienced players, it may be advisable that the bat should rest lightly on the ground.

This mirror practice introduces a basic model for developing stance, with a hint at the off-drive, but, as Sir Stanley Jackson did with his mirror golf, you need to refer constantly to text-books to make sure that what you are practising is correct, and, again, never be afraid to ask if something is troubling you or there is something you cannot understand. Cricketers are very helpful to each other. Even at county level opponents will tell each other what is being done wrongly when one or other is having a bad patch.

It is possible to generalise about stance for batting. It is less easy to do so for bowling because

Aggression and attack in bowling. Chris Cowdrey at medium pace.

1   2

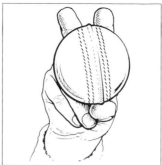
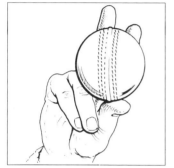
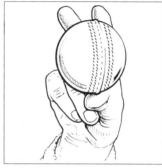

Demonstrating (top left) seam bowling grip, (right) grip for seamer, seam up. (Below left) grip for inswinger (right) grip for outswinger.

3

4

there is a difference between the seam bowler and the spin bowler. There are one or two basics, however, with which your mirror can help you.

What is reflected to you in your mirror is your moment of delivering the ball. Is the front shoulder pointing towards the batsman and the head looking straight down the wicket at him? The position of the head must be maintained even as the body pivots at the moment of releasing the ball. You can check, too, that you are in close to the stumps, that your arm is high and that your grip on the ball is as you want it to be. For quicker bowlers, the seam is usually held so that it is vertical; for spinners it is held horizontally so that the fingers can work upon it. In your mirror, you are able to check not only that your grip is correct at the point of delivery, but also the position of the wrist, the arm, the head and all else.

The wicket-keeper, too, can determine his basic stance by working with the mirror. The squatting position should be comfortable with the weight on the balls of the feet. The eyes and head should be still and level looking straight ahead at the bowler and the ball.

Alan Knott, the wicket-keeper takes up his stance. Comfort and balance are all-important.

The hands are together, the palms facing outwards and the backs of the gloves touching the ground. The fingers are pointing down in anticipation of taking the ball. The balance must be right, and by rising as if to take the ball, you can develop an easy rhythm which is so necessary to good wicket-keeping.

BOOKS

So far we have looked at what can be done with the aid of a mirror, preferably, of course, a full-length mirror, but it has also been stressed that there is a need to refer to a text-book or coaching manual. There are several coaching manuals on the market, but we would recommend three above the others. The first is *The Skills of Cricket* by Keith Andrew, and it is published in a paperback edition by Crowood Press at £4.95. Keith Andrew is the head of the National Cricket Association whose address was given in the second chapter. This is the association that gives the greatest help to young cricketers in the organisation of coaching courses and very much else. Keith himself is among the top coaches in the world. A former wicket-keeper for England and Northamptonshire, he writes simply and clearly for young people as well as older people, and his book is easy to follow for those who would practise in front of the mirror.

Keith Andrew has also provided the technical coaching points in another highly recommended publication, *The Test and County Cricket Board Guide to Better Cricket* by Vic Marks, the Somerset and England cricketer, published by Octopus Books at £12.95. This is a much more lavish book than the first recommended. It is a coaching book for anyone 'between 7 and 97 who is remotely interested in the game' and is highly readable, with comments on style and technique from some of the leading players of the day.

Of a more traditional nature is *Complete Cricket Coaching* by Frank Tyson, a great fast bowler for England. This is published by Pelham Books at £12.95. The diagrams are good; the advice is sound.

Although prices and publishers have been stated

Ian Botham, the great all-rounder, attacking with the ball . . .

. . . and with the bat.

in each case, all of these books should be available at your local library; nor are they the only books of value. The point is that you do need the help of a manual when you are trying to establish good *habits* by your mirror practice. There is no good to be gained from practising strokes and bowling actions wrongly.

No one is suggesting that you can learn cricket from a book or without hitting a ball, but the book and the mirror can provide steps along the way. Nor would one suggest that every cricketer rigidly follows a coaching manual. The great player masters technique, but he shapes it to his own ends and his own personality.

The best example of this is to be seen in the cricket of Ian Botham. Botham is an attacking cricketer in all that he does, batting, bowling and fielding. He hits the ball with tremendous power, and sometimes plays extravagant and audacious strokes. He tries for so much variety in his bowling that he has often taken wickets with what many would consider were bad balls, simply because the batsman had no idea what to expect next. At slip, he stands closer than the text-book would recommend, yet he has pulled off some astonishing catches. One would not ask a young cricketer to model himself on Botham, for none could play in quite his style, yet Botham himself had his training in the hardest of schools, the ground staff at Lord's where discipline is strict and strong technique thoroughly inculcated.

Similarly, the genius of Abdul Qadir, the great Pakistan spin bowler, is not that he has perfected the art of the leg-break just from the text-book. Once he had mastered the basic technique he developed and experimented within the bounds of his own ability and imagination. To the leg-break he added the conventional googly (the off-break with the leg-break action), the top-spinner and a googly which differed in action from the first. His bowling is successful at the highest level because he is ever thoughtful and inventive, but also because the skill has been honed from a sound basis.

Thinking and talking are an important part of cricket, for few games give as much cause for discussion or have a greater tradition. It is necessary for every cricketer, however humble, to be a part of that tradition, and he should let the history of the game enfold him. No sport has so vast or good a literature as cricket, and the close season is an excellent time to catch up with the reading of the game's classics. The point of this is not simply to become acquainted with facts and figures and the great names of the past and present, but to become more involved with the game and to obtain a greater understanding of it. The better you understand a game, the better you will play it. You will learn the language of cricket more quickly by submerging yourself in its literature.

Opposite: Abdul Qadir, the great leg-spin bowler. He has an infinite variety of deliveries.

It is as well to start with your own county or area, for you will quickly realise that you are part of a brotherhood that has been in existence for nearly three hundred years and that however slight a player you may think yourself, you have a contribution to make to a great tradition.

A story is told of how Richard Hutton, son of the great Sir Leonard Hutton, used to take a copy of Lord Hawke's memoirs on tour with him and read from them in such a way to other members of the party as to bring them close to tears. Richard Hutton was himself an England cricketer, but he was also part of Yorkshire tradition, and Lord Hawke was the captain who revived Yorkshire cricket and led it to glory a hundred years ago.

The suggestion that reading about cricket is a worthy part of preparing for the game may seem trivial to some, but essentially cricket is a game where talking, debating and reminiscing play an important part, and you need to be well informed to participate in the discussion. There are hours of pleasure ahead. Read widely. Read anything. You will soon discover that which gives you the most satisfaction and that which you can discard.

VIDEOS

In recent times there has been a tendency for people to watch rather than to read, and the television and the video have played an increasingly large part in people's lives. The advent of video has been something of a boon to cricket, both in recording the great feats of great players and in providing material which can be used for studying the game and learning its skills.

Although not everyone has access to a video recorder/player, if it is possible to have the use of one there are some very entertaining and useful videos to be watched. On the historical side, there are tapes of the tied Test match between Australia and West Indies, the great England–Australia series in 1981 in which Botham performed amazing deeds, and many other famous matches and series. There is a video showing the great batsmen and bowlers from W.G. Grace onwards, and there is another showing Don Bradman in all his glory. But of most use for the winter months are those videos which are instructional and which will help you to develop your techniques in preparation for the coming season. Foremost among these is a series of five tapes produced by the National Cricket Association and their chief executive, Keith Andrew, with the aid of the National Westminster Bank.

There are two tapes on batting, two on bowling and one on fielding. The series is introduced by Sir Garfield Sobers, and the commentary and explanation is by Tony Lewis. None of the five tapes runs for more than 25 minutes so that there is just enough information to be absorbed and not so much that you become numbed.

The first of the two video tapes on batting concerns forward play and is demonstrated by Graham Gooch. The second demonstrates back play and shows Allan Lamb displaying his talents. The two bowling videos concern pace bowling and spin bowling. Ian Botham and Norman Cowans demonstrate the art of pace bowling, while the guiles of spin are revealed by John Emburey (off-break), Phil Edmonds (left-arm) and Abdul Qadir (leg-break). Fielding and wicket-keeping instruction is given by David Gower and Bob Taylor. It will be realised that the demonstration of all the aspects of the game is in the hands of the most capable players in modern cricket.

The series is called *This Game of Cricket* and the set of five tapes costs £75, but it is not suggested that you dash out to buy a set. Most libraries now offer a video-lending service which concentrates on lending videos of an educational and instructional nature. *This Game of Cricket*, of course, falls into that category, and even if your local library does not have them in stock, it should be able to obtain them for you from another branch.

WINTER FITNESS

The hints given so far as to how to work at your game during the close season or when you are not playing are all of a rather passive nature – standing in front of a mirror, reading, watching videos – but it is unlikely that such a programme would suit someone who is anxious to be doing things and is energetic by nature.

We shall come later to some ideas on fitness, but it is obvious that a cricketer cannot hope to go straight out to play at the end of April unless he has kept himself in some sort of trim during the winter, and, at a time when games are becoming increasingly more competitive, fitness is essential. If you play soccer, rugby, squash, badminton or some other sport in the winter, then you are likely to maintain a good level of fitness so that you are not asking too much of your body when summer comes. If you do not, then it is very necessary that you do some light jogging and exercise in the period leading up to the cricket season and during the season itself.

This applies especially to older players, and to those who, through pressure of business or for other reasons, have not played for three or four years and are returning to the game. At first it will seem easy to pick up a bat again and to recommence a career in club or village cricket as if there has been no gap, but the muscles will rebel. If you play on a Sunday, you will find that your body may not recover until the following Thursday, that your muscles will be stiff and that you could be in considerable pain and find it difficult to move. It is a fact that as you grow older,

It is important for all to perform simple exercise, both in the lead up to the season and at other times you need to play regularly and exercise regularly. But it is important for all to perform simple exercise both in the lead-up to the season and at other times.

Jogging has become such a common feature of our lives that one is almost ashamed to suggest it, but it is an invaluable means of keeping in trim. Jogging is simply what it states, a light trot at a pace which is comfortable for the jogger for a distance and length of time that suits him. Jogging is not preparation for a marathon, doing as many miles as possible at as fast a pace as possible. It is an exercise to keep muscles warm and the body fitter for the exertions that you may put on it in another field, in this case cricket. Do not rush at it. Go gently and increase pace and distance as and when it suits you. You are not trying to test your body against the elements.

Again one would suggest that older players who have done no exercise for some time should approach jogging with caution. Begin by walking round the park or the block regularly and increase the pace gradually until you feel capable of jogging lightly. Treat it gently. Do not over-exert yourself, and most importantly make sure you wear good training shoes.

Jogging or, if you have it, using an exercise bike is an admirable way of getting in trim and warming the body. You can supplement this with light and simple exercises such as knee bending and press-ups or the gentle rotation of the arms. Do not push yourself to do things that are beyond your capabilities. Work towards tasks and exercise gradually.

We have already mentioned press-ups (on the bedroom carpet) and this is an exercise which suggests strength. Strength in the sense of great muscular development is not essential in cricket, but the de-

velopment of strength in the hands and wrists and, in
particular, the top hand is very neces-   **Strength in the hands and wrists should**
sary and must be worked on.   **be developed to gain control**

A right-handed batsman has his left hand as the
top hand on the bat; for a left-handed batsman the
top hand is the right hand. Invariably, this top hand
is the weaker hand. It is the one that you do not write
with, and it is the one with which you tend to do less,
yet it is the hand with which you swing the bat. The
bottom hand is for guidance. It is the top hand which,
in effect, holds the bat.

The natural weakness in the top hand is a main
reason for batsmen not playing straight, for losing
control of the bat and not playing through the line of
the ball as you bring the bat down, yet this weakness
can be rectified by a simple exercise which you can
do as you travel to work or school by bus, by train
or when walking.

You need an old squash ball or something similar
– a small, hard, rubber ball. All that you need to do is
to keep the ball in your pocket and knead it constantly
when you are not doing anything else. The consistent
opening and closing of the hand over the rubber ball,
which will give a little at the pressure, will begin to
give you more *feeling* in the hand and eventually the
hand will grow stronger.

The small rubber ball is not only of advantage for
strengthening the top hand for batting, it is also most
effective for helping a bowler to get easier manipula-
tion of his fingers, most necessary for the spinner.
Many of the great spin bowlers have told how they
have carried a squash ball in their pocket and, at odd
moments, have flicked it and spun it between their
fingers. It is all part of getting the feel of the ball and
of gaining that mastery over it which is the desire of
every bowler.

The bowler wants to feel that he can place the
ball where he likes and do with it what he wants,
turn it, swing it or seam it. This mastery is generally
summed up in the press by the word 'control'. The
basis of control is to have a command over length so

Derek Underwood.
His relentless
accuracy frustrated
many batsmen.

that you are able to pitch the ball on the exact spot you want. A consistent command of length does not come easily, and it demands application and self-discipline. It is something that can be practised in those times when you are not playing.

It is a simple enough exercise. You need some space – a back garden, an alley-way – any spot that is not too inhabited and where you won't have to go too far to fetch the ball. Fix a sheet of newspaper or a handkerchief to the ground (stones at each corner will suffice) so that you can bowl at it from as near to 22 yards as possible. It does not matter if your space allows you only some 10 to 15 yards in which to bowl. The important thing is for you to keep bowling the ball on to the piece of paper so that you develop a rhythm of accuracy.

Success will not be as easy or as consistent as you may think, but once you feel you have total command and can pitch the ball on the sheet of newspaper nineteen times out of twenty, fold the paper in half and give yourself a smaller target at which to aim. In his bowling, Derek Underwood relied not only on his ability to turn the ball sharply, but also on his relentless accuracy. He frustrated batsmen, turned them to despair, because he could consistently pitch the ball in the most awkward spot.

It is not just the bowler who can gain outdoor practice on his own. There is a method which a batsman can employ that enables him to hit the ball and practise his shots without the chore of having to run miles to recover the ball. Fit a ball into the toe of an old sock and hang it on a clothes lines. It must be tightly tied because you are going to hit the ball, and it must be suspended at the right height for you to hit. A clothes line is the obvious choice, but any way of supporting the sock so that it hangs at the right height is satisfactory. With the ball suspended in front of you, you can position yourself to play a variety of shots. The slight adjustment in your own position can make it legitimate to practise both leg-side and off-side shots, for you are able to determine where you would like the ball to pitch.

The material in this section is simply a list of suggestions and hints of what can be done to keep in practice and help develop your game in idle moments in the close season. It would be unwise to fill every minute with watching, practising or reading about cricket. Staleness is a big enemy, and most people are better for coming to the game refreshed after a few weeks' rest. In the professional game, most players feel like a holiday at the end of the season and intense county practice does not begin until a few weeks before the beginning of the next season. So it should be with net practice.

NET PRACTICE

Most clubs will try to arrange nets from the time that the evenings become longer in early April, weather permitting, but many are now finding it possible to arrange indoor net practice from January until the

Practice makes perfect.

beginning of the season. Whatever is available, make use of it, and use it wisely. Enjoy it.

The hints given here are solitary exercises. None of them is a substitute for good net practice, just as net practice can never be as good as practice in the middle. One of the benefits of net practice is that it brings members of a team together; one of its disadvantages is the failure of some club members to take it seriously enough.

There is a tendency to treat batting in the nets as a happy-go-lucky slog, which is wrong, for such an attitude can bring bad habits. Certainly, you should not be afraid to hit the ball in the nets, nor should you be afraid to try shots of which you are not confident. This is the purpose of the practice, but it is essential that you realise what you are doing wrong, and right, and that you work away to correct faults that you have. In this respect, the benefit of nets being a team gathering is apparent. However old you are, and however experienced, you can still be assisted by other people. At Kent, Bob Woolmer used to be on hand to point out errors and technical weaknesses; not everyone has the benefit of such a coach, but it is still possible to give and to receive help from each other. Always listen to advice, even if you ultimately reject it.

A batsman will soon realise that he is playing and missing outside the off stump, but he may well not know why. A colleague may be able to diagnose the fault straight away, and it may be something simple such as when the batsman is playing forward to the off and his front leg is coming straight down the wicket rather than down and across to meet the pitch of the ball. Observations on grip, stance, balance and the placement of the feet can be made by colleagues and be of great assistance.

Bowlers are not often quite so well served in net practice as are batsmen. This applies particularly to indoor nets where the bowler's run-up is restricted. Nevertheless, it is in the nets that a bowler has the best opportunity to improve his control of length. It is also in the nets that the bowler can experiment in a way which he is reluctant to do in a match for fear of what might happen.

We are thinking especially of the young leg-spinner who is trying to develop the googly, or the medium-pace bowler who wants to try to add the away-swinger to his repertoire. Both deliveries need a grip and an action which can be perfected only with much practice. Even then, there is no guarantee that things will come right when you try them in the middle, but at least you will have gained the confidence to try if you have once got them right in the nets.

What should have been made clear in this section is that you can develop your knowledge and skill at cricket even when you are not playing. Practice, with and without other people, exercises to increase manipulative ability, studying and reading about techniques, learning something of the history of the game and of the great players, all these are things which can be done in the close season or in those hours when you are not actually playing. They are all valuable occupations, for cricket is a thinking game, and the more you immerse yourself in it, the more you will understand and the more you will enjoy it.

4 FOOD AND FITNESS

Few subjects have commanded more public attention and debate in the last ten years than that of food diet. As well as resulting in lobbying to persuade people not to smoke and to drink less alcohol, the concern for the nation's health has reached the point of suggesting that some form of control should be exerted over what people eat. 'You are what you eat' is the slogan, and with the amount of 'fast food', 'junk' food in the eyes of many, which is being consumed today, what we are may not be too happy a thought.

Allied to this concern has been the boom in health foods, organic products – naturally grown and untreated by chemicals – and in controlled diets. Several cricketers have even been part of an advertising campaign for one special form of diet, but more about this later.

Before we begin to worry too much about food and drink we should look at the habits of some of the great players of the past. In the earliest days of county cricket it was customary for the gentlemen to take a long break, dinner rather than lunch, and they would leave the ground and go to a nearby hotel where they would eat and drink before returning for the afternoon session of play.

In the early part of this century, W.G. Grace, the greatest of cricketers, was renowned for his eating habits. Major James Gilman, who opened the batting with Grace for the London County side at Crystal

Palace in the match against the first West Indian side to tour this country, told how W.G. 'was very keen on the catering' and that he had 'a sumptuous lunch, with hock and claret on the table. He had a real whack of the roast, followed by a big lump of cheese. He also tackled his whisky and seltzer, which was always his drink.'

It should be added that although the 'Old Man' scored 71, he was out shortly after this particular feast.

One of the greatest of fast-medium-pace bowlers, Maurice Tate, is said to have always had a couple of pints of Guinness at lunch-time to 'recharge his batteries' for a long stint of bowling in the afternoon.

Cricket has changed much since the days of Grace and Tate, however, and no player today could behave as they did. One should remember, too, that *great* players are a law unto themselves and are capable of behaving in a way different from lesser mortals. One is reminded of a story concerning the man who is possibly the finest golfer that England has ever produced, Henry Cotton. Having won all that there was to be won, he was drinking in the bar of the clubhouse one evening when he was approached by a young man who apologised courteously for interrupting him, and asked Cotton if he could give him any advice as an enthusiastic young professional. 'Yes,' said Cotton, pointing to the glass of whisky that the young man was drinking, 'don't drink that.' The young player was somewhat taken aback, for, as he pointed out, Cotton himself was drinking whisky. 'Yes,' said the great man, 'but I'm Henry Cotton, and I've already won the Open and played in the Ryder Cup.'

This is not a story of arrogance, but rather a reminder that when we watch players like Gooch, Gatting, Botham and Gower in action we are inclined to forget the discipline and hard work that has gone into making them what they are. None of these players has reached the top of his profession by over-indulging in his days of apprenticeship. The advent of one-day cricket has placed a greater importance than ever before on physical fitness, for the demands of instant cricket are for athletic fielding and quick reflexes. Eating habits are a part of fitness, but they vary greatly.

Very few players will eat a large meal during a match. Many will eat only fruit at lunch-time, and **Eating habits are a part of fitness** several, if the lunch interval falls when they are batting, will eat nothing at all. In a hot summer, salad dishes are invariably favourite. Certainly, if one could give general advice about eating lunch and tea during a match, it would be to eat sparingly and certainly to avoid stodgy foods.

Among the leading players, Graham Gooch, who used to have a whole catalogue of things that he would not eat, is very careful with his food, for he is a fitness fanatic and is most anxious not to carry surplus weight. Even more fastidious is Alan Knott; no better wicket-keeper has ever played for England.

Knott was totally dedicated in everything that he did relating to cricket, and this included his diet. He sought the advice of an American health expert who advised him that if he wanted to obtain the maximum

Alan Knott makes a spectacular dive down the leg side to catch left-handed Rodney Marsh, the Australian wicket-keeper/batsman.

energy output, he should eat only natural foods. He has maintained a strict adherence to the principle since receiving that advice. He never eats meat and cheese at the same meal. There must be no artificial preservatives in any food that he eats – a fact that can be discerned from the ingredients label on the packaging. He takes his tea with honey, and he rarely ate anything but fruit or drank anything more than milk during a match.

Some may consider Knott's diet to be extreme, but it came about as the result of careful thought and balance as to what was best for him, that he may get the best out of his game. It would not suit everybody, particularly those who have another job of work to do for five or six days a week and for whom cricket is simply a relaxation at weekends, but one would suggest that it is advisable to watch what one eats more carefully than most people tend to do.

The main problem is the pace at which most of us live. We seem to be constantly in a hurry so that we have little time to take enough care over our meals. If this is the case, then it is better to have fruit and yoghurt for lunch than a beefburger, the ingredients of which may be dubious. It is undeniable that the fresher and more natural the food, the better we are for it. After a long journey and a tiring day at work or school, many take the easy way out and go for convenience foods – pre-packaged, frozen or tinned food. This is unavoidable in some cases, but every effort should be made to eat fresh vegetables.

There are other simple dietary rules that one can follow. One should avoid fried food as much as possible, and where a meal can be either fried or grilled, choose the latter. The first method puts fat in; the second takes it out and uses the fat within the food itself in the cooking process. Take time over eating. Eating should be a pleasure, and pleasures should be lingered over. Do not rush a meal. Give yourself a chance to digest. Life is fast enough anyway.

It is true that much of this advice on food is

common sense, but many of us do often lapse in that area. This also applies to drinking habits: a doctor may suggest that one whisky, one pint of beer or a glass of wine each day may be good for an older player, but when the number of glasses or pints begins to increase it becomes harmful.

The question of liquid intake during a match is important because it replaces energy which has been expended. In Australia, where it can be far hotter than it ever is in England, it is customary for players to drink Staminade in drink intervals. This looks something like washing-up liquid, but it has a glucose ingredient which restores what has been lost in exerting and sweating in the sun. Glucozade is a near equivalent in England, but a refreshing drink with fruit and limited sugar content will suffice.

Food and drink all comes down to a matter of common sense, and as in all such matters, the best thing to do is to consult an expert. This must be done when it comes to a question of dieting. If you feel that you are carrying too much weight, and most of us are, and have a need to reduce in order to feel fitter, speak to your doctor and ask his or her advice. Much depends on age and height, and the doctor will be able to tell you exactly what steps you should take and what is necessary and healthy. Do not rush out to follow some patented, expensive course. What is suitable for a middle-aged woman may be far from suitable for an aspiring young cricketer, or even an older one who would like to start playing again.

You need to be patient and to accept your own natural physical limitations. Although we would perhaps like to, we cannot all look like David Gower. The answer is to make the very best of what we have been given.

If any single aspect of the game has changed dramatically over the past fifteen to twenty years, it is the professional cricketer's attitude towards physical training and preparation before the season begins, and, indeed, his desire to keep in trim throughout the season. This changed attitude has filtered down

Opposite: David Gower, a batsman of charm and easy grace, the result of perfect timing.

to club, village and school level where it is now being increasingly realised that cricket is a game that demands something more than just picking up a bat or a ball and playing for a few afternoons during the summer.

Cricket is a game that demands something more than just picking up a bat or a ball and playing

ONE-DAY CRICKET

Cricket must once more thank the limited-over game for this change in attitude. Twenty years ago, players would simply arrive for a pre-season net, have a bat, a bowl and perhaps a bit of fielding practice. There was little concern for what any of them had been doing in the winter or, indeed, for the rigours of the weeks ahead. Before 1963 when the Gillette Cup (now the NatWest Bank Trophy) came into being, cricket was a more leisurely game than it is today.

The one-day game brought large crowds back to matches and greater financial rewards to players, and therefore increased their responsibilities to spectators, sponsors and those who run the game. When you play in front of a capacity crowd at Canterbury in the quarter-final of the Benson and Hedges Cup or NatWest Trophy, the last thing you want to do is to fail for lack of physical fitness or alertness. Those looking on will soon let you know if you are falling short of expectations.

One-day cricket has made it imperative that fields-men are alert, that dives are now made to stop balls that once would have been waved at and allowed to pass on for four. At club and village level, the growth of leagues and the increase in competitive cricket have produced a similar keener edge in the fielding. League cricket has many critics, as has the one-day game for professionals, but none can deny that, in both cases, fielding has become infinitely sharper and better than it was in the past.

In batting, too, in the basic art of running between the wickets, there has been a vast improvement. Where once a single was sauntered, two runs are now scampered. Every run run, every run stopped, has become vital; and that can only be good for the game.

The extra physical demands on speed and stamina have made physical preparation more and more important, yet even now it would be arrogant to suggest that the average cricketer, at whatever level, is as fit as his counterpart in soccer. Graham Gooch is one who trains with a professional football side in the winter, in his case West Ham United, and the improvement in his fitness over the past ten years has been extraordinary. Others have followed their own individual training programmes. Again, Alan Knott, ever his own man, is a case in point.

Knott is not a naturally gifted athlete; he is not a supple or loose-limbed mover. For this reason, he evolved a pattern of constant exercises which concentrated on stretching the groin and hamstring muscles to keep himself lithe. These exercises were strongly allied to his wicket-keeping duties, as were his diving practices. He would dive to left and right alternately, gently at first, but with ever-increasing difficulty. In this way, he believed he developed rhythm. The proof of his physical training could be seen in his performance.

This section has so far mentioned some specialised training routines. It now moves on to concentrate more on the general.

As in so many other sports, cricketers at one time could understand physical preparation only in terms of running round the field. They thought initially that a few laps would be sufficient. Assuredly, running is important in building up stamina, but it is not everyone's idea of enjoyment, and the more you enjoy your training, the more you are likely to get out of it. As well as traditional training, Viv Richards places great stress on swimming as one of the means by which he gets fit and keeps fit. He also emphasizes exercises which help the development of the abdominal muscles.

The general training programme for a county involves some three to four miles of running twice per week in the couple of months before the season begins to get the body warm and ready for action.

Fitness has become vital to the professional cricketer. Bob Willis does leg exercises with Bob Thomas.

The long-distance running builds up endurance and is the basis of the training that comes later. As the season nears we introduce sprints, but it should be pointed out that we move into these gradually. It would be unwise and dangerous to go flat out right from the start. Then come the exercises which have become a common sight wherever cricketers are at work – the stretching exercises. Few will forget the sight of Bob Willis, more than six feet six inches tall, standing with one leg placed on the shoulder of Bob Thomas, the England and Warwickshire physiotherapist. It was part of Willis's stretching exercises, and they were most important to him.

One can think of no example of a cricketer whose dedicated physical preparation for the game has stood him in better stead than Bob Willis, who survived a series of injuries which would have ended the careers of lesser men. Like most players, he was emphatic about the need for mental discipline.

Mental discipline is vital in any sport, but none

more so than cricket. For the weekend cricketer or the young person just beginning in the game, mental discipline is best summed up as having the right attitude. It covers a wide area – the determination to set yourself standards and work to them; the relaxed, yet alert, approach to the game; the ability to pick yourself up when things go wrong; and the belief that a game can always be won or saved. One need only look at the results of some of the one-day finals at Lord's over the past few years to realise how important the last quality is – Kent nearly snatched victory over Middlesex in the Benson and Hedges Cup Final of 1986 when Steve Marsh pulled a ball into the Grandstand for six; England did beat Australia when Allan Lamb hit fourteen off the last over; Middlesex did beat Essex by 4 runs after all had seemed lost in the Benson and Hedges Cup Final of 1983.

The right attitude to the game is greatly facilitated if the body is fit. It is easier to lose heart if you are tired; easier to drive yourself on if you are fit and healthy.

The right attitude to the game is greatly facilitated if the body is fit

The longer-distance running and the sprints to build up stamina and speed need little explanation. For the rest you need a little guidance, although you may soon come to work out your own programme.

If you have access to a gymnasium where you can work at very little cost, so much the better. For over thirty years one of the most profitable forms of individual training has been circuit training. In effect, you test yourself against the circuit of exercises demanded to see the maximum number of times that you can do sit-ups, press-ups, arm-stretches, step-ups etc. Then you go round the circuit as often as possible doing half your maximum each time. You will soon build up strength.

Stretching exercises are the ones we have emphasized as being most important to cricketers. There is a variety of such exercises, from the simple swinging of the arms to left and right while you stand with legs wide apart and feet flat on the floor, to the exercise where you place the feet together, put the left foot

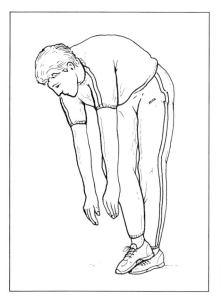

Stretching exercises.

over the right and press down ten times to the floor. You should keep the back arched and stretch slowly with the hands pointing downwards. Obviously, you then repeat the exercise with the right foot over the left. This is an excellent exercise for the hamstrings.

Such exercises as these and the circuit training really need the advice of an expert such as the warden at the sports centre, the person in charge of the local gymnasium, or simply a physical education teacher who plays for your local club or village side, or whom you know. The point is that physical preparation is not an area that you should rush into unthinkingly. It is as dangerous for the young person to leap into a series of unscheduled exercises, even though he is fit, as it is for an older person who has done little physical activity for several years. A younger body has different needs from an older one so advice should be sought.

One thing is certain: the older a sportsman gets, the more regular his training needs to be. The big mistake that is so often made is that as a cricketer gets older he decides to play less when, in fact, he should be playing more. Richard Hadlee left county

Richard Hadlee.
Dedication,
application, fitness
and economy
of style.

cricket at the end of the 1987 season because he felt that at his age, thirty-six, he could no longer cope with the extra training that was needed to get him through an English season. He no longer relished pounding the streets at six o'clock in the morning, which he regarded as essential if he were to maintain the high standard which he had set himself and which people had come to expect from him. Richard is a serious man, and his exceptional success at Test and county level as an all-round cricketer has been achieved only after considerable hard work over a period of years.

It was interesting in 1987 to watch the Nottingham-

shire side during the last month of the season when they were close to capturing the Britannic Assurance County Championship. Even after a few hours in the field they could be seen, at the close of play, trotting round the ground three or four times in their eagerness to maintain their standard of fitness for the last weeks of the season, the time when many begin to flag. Clive Rice, the Nottinghamshire captain, and Richard Hadlee are both strong advocates of physical fitness, which is why both have lasted so long in the game at the highest level.

One vital factor in the matter of fitness is to keep the muscles warm. A gentle warm-up before fielding, bowling or batting is essential. To rush headlong into an activity is to court disaster. There is the story of the ex-England footballer who joined a Third Division side, but was unable to play for several weeks because of an injury. When he was finally fit to play he ran out of the tunnel on to the pitch and wanted to leap into the action so quickly that he pulled a muscle in the pre-match practice and had to be substituted before the kick-off. That turned out to be his sole appearance for the club.

It is as vital to warm down as it is to warm up, which is why a bowler must put on a sweater at the end of each over, why a batsman will shower and change after a long innings when he gets to the pavilion, and why it is never sensible to stand about for long periods in the clothes in which you have been fielding for three or four hours.

Muscle warmth is important, for when muscles become cold and you try to use them they pull and strain, and your cricket is over for a while.

A simple regard for the health of the mind and the body is the basis for success and more enjoyment in the game.

Opposite: Clive Rice is a strong advocate of physical fitness, which is why he has lasted so long in the game.

5 THE LANGUAGE OF CRICKET

All sports have their own language. In most it is jargon rather than language, but cricket is a sport rich in literature and therefore in language itself. As we have said, it is a game in which discussion and debate tend to play an important part. The newcomer, of whatever age, can become involved in these debates or develop a desire to read about the game or listen to a broadcast commentary on radio or television of a Test or county match. Enthusiastic and eager to learn more, he may be baffled and bemused by the battery of words with which he is bombarded.

Leg-break and leg-cutter, swing and seam, military medium – the terms tumble over each other, and the uninitiated enthusiast can be left perplexed by the mysteries of this game which, in other ways, he finds so beautifully simple. There is either no one to ask, or a reluctance to ask, the way through this labyrinth, so perhaps a little guidance may be of use.

Like all language, the language of cricket is a living thing. Words change according to their use; words die; words are born. The 'draw' and the 'Harrow drive' are shots which have gone out of practice so the words themselves have become obsolete. The reverse sweep, on the other hand, is a term which has been resuscitated.

This is interesting to note, for the reverse sweep is one shot which has been blamed on the one-day game. The normal sweep is the shot which sweeps the ball with a horizontal bat into the area between square leg and long leg. It is played to slow bowling pitched around leg stump. It was used a great deal by Denis Compton, but in today's game it has become criticised, although Graham Gooch uses it to good effect and John Emburey has his own peculiar version with which he scores many runs.

It is a dangerous shot in that in sweeping across the ball you have more chance of missing it, and you need to be very sure where it pitches. The reverse sweep is even more dangerous for, in effect, the right-handed batsman becomes effectively left-handed, turning the wrists over and sweeping from leg to off. Ian Botham uses it often, but he is a law unto himself, a player to be enjoyed rather than imitated, and Mike Gatting has scored many runs with the shot. Gatting, however, was out in the World Cup Final against Australia when he tried to reverse sweep Allan Border's first delivery and lobbed the ball up in the air to the wicket-keeper.

In limited-over cricket, there is pressure on batsmen to score runs quickly, and therefore we improvise, but the reverse sweep is not a shot that should be

Botham the unorthodox. The reverse sweep. Not a shot for beginners.

embraced by someone starting the game or returning to it after some years' absence. It is not, however, a new shot, nor a new term. W.G. Grace's brother, E.M., a fine batsman who played for England, was said to have played the reverse sweep, as did Percy Fender, the Surrey captain of the 1920s who hit the fastest century in first-class cricket, in 35 minutes against Northamptonshire in 1920.

Nevertheless, the reverse sweep is not a stroke that is found in many coaching manuals. As a term, it has something of a disreputable ring about it for many people, particularly the purists and traditionalists.

THE LANGUAGE OF BOWLING

Most batting terms are self-explanatory and are soon picked up. It is the language of bowling which causes young people the greatest problems. The basis of slow bowling is simple enough. There are two types of right-arm slow bowler: the off-bowler and the leg-break bowler.

The off-break is the ball which spins into the batsman from the off. The break or spin is usually achieved by the fingers, which impart the spin or turn to the ball. The off-break can also be called the break-back.

The leg-break turns from leg to off, and therefore tends to move across or away from the batsman. The spin on the leg-break is usually imparted by the movement of the wrist at the moment of delivery, which is why leg-break bowlers, few in number today, are known as wrist-spinners and off-break bowlers as finger-spinners.

This is relatively simple and straightforward. The more complex vocabulary occurs when we speak of the variety in the slow bowler's repertoire.

There is the top-spinner, which is bowled by the wrist-spinner or leg-break bowler, where the ball is made to go straight on rather than turn and which deceives the batsman by its extra pace so that it hurries off the pitch. There is the googly, a famous part of the leg-break bowler's armoury, wherein he bowls

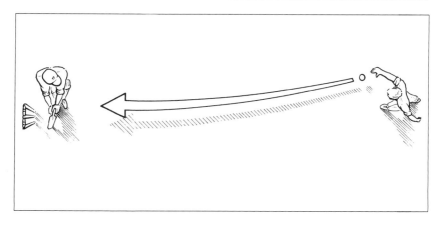

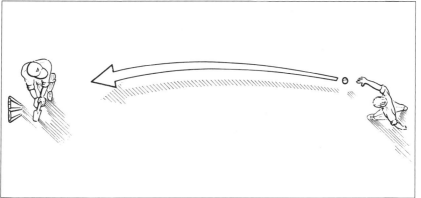

what looks as if it will be a leg-break, for it is delivered with what the batsman thinks is the same action, but turns out to be an off-break, that is it spins the opposite way from that expected.

Most people have heard and understand the meaning of the googly, if not how to spot it, yet in Australia it is still known as the 'bosie' after the man who invented it, the Middlesex all-rounder B.J.T. Bosanquet.

Another version of the top-spinner is the flipper. This is, in fact, a slow delivery but will deceive in that it tends to hustle through rather low in height.

A great leg-spinner such as Abdul Qadir presents a fascinating study if you watch him go through his repertoire of leg-breaks, googlies, top-spinners and

Ball trajectory of, top, the off-break and, below, the leg-break.

flippers, and much else of his own invention.

The off-break bowler is much more common in county cricket. John Emburey, Eddie Hemmings and Vic Marks are three who have proved that the off-break bowler can be as effective in limited-over cricket as in Championship matches, and Emburey and Hemmings were two of the main reasons that England reached the World Cup Final.

An off-break bowler varies the way in which he bowls according to the context of the match. In a limited-over game, he tends to bowl with a flat trajectory which spears the ball into the batsman and restricts his opportunity to score. In a three-day game, and, if he is wise, in club and village cricket, he will give the ball air, that is to say he will bowl with a high, looping trajectory which will encourage the batsman to hit the ball in the air. This control over trajectory is the off-break bowler's weapon, for with it he can deceive the batsman as to line, length and pace of the ball.

The floater is the well-flighted ball, tossed into the air and curving, floating, deceptively towards or away from the batsman.

The slow left-arm bowler's natural delivery is a leg-break. The delivery he bowls that turns the other way, in fact his googly, is called the chinaman, although one should add that this term is being used in an increasingly wider context so that it is difficult on occasions to know quite what it means.

This should have taken you through some of the maze of words used about the slow bowler. Whatever the bowler, be he slow, medium or fast, he can bowl a batsman out with a yorker.

In reality, a bowler can only *attempt* to bowl a yorker, for the delivery becomes a yorker only if the batsman is deceived, and if, deceived by the length and believing the ball to be a full toss or a half-volley, he allows the full-length delivery to pass underneath his bat as it pitches. A batsman can be bowled by a yorker only if he tries to hit at it, unless delivered at great pace.

John Emburey, orthodox and economic.

The yorker is more the weapon of the fast and medium-pace bowler than of the slow bowler. English cricket thrives on the medium-pace bowler. Few men are gifted with the physical ability to bowl fast, and the medium-pacer has the stamina and accuracy to make the backbone, the stock bowler of an attack.

There has been a fashion to disparage the medium-pace bowler, forgetting the greatness of players like Maurice Tate, Alec Bedser, Tom Cartwright, and even Derek Underwood whom many club cricketers would describe as fast. The term military medium is used, again somewhat disparagingly, to describe a steady medium-pace bowler, efficient and reliable, who bowls with seam up and relies on accuracy rather than movement so that he tends to restrict rather than to get the batsman out.

The medium-pacer is a seam bowler (although not in Underwood's case). He holds the ball with

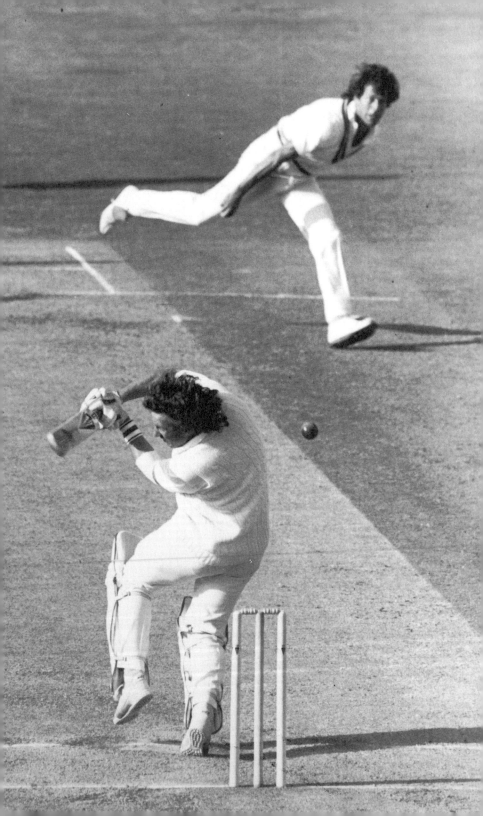

the seam straight between the fingers so that it *may* swing either way in the air and will move off the seam in either direction when the seam of the ball hits the pitch.

Swing is what is achieved through the air by the quicker bowler; seam is the reaction off the pitch. The art of swing bowling is a most complex affair, dependent on many factors and commanded by very few. The medium-pacer's main offensive weapons are his leg-cutter and off-cutter. They are equivalent to the leg-break and off-break, but they are achieved at a brisker pace and by a different method. The hand is jerked as the fingers come across the ball, and on pitching, the ball cuts in from off or leg.

Apart from his swing and movement, the *fast* bowler has become renowned (or notorious, depending on which side you are on) for the bouncer, or bumper. Below top pace it has little value except to provide the batsman with the opportunity to hit four runs. It is a fast delivery that pitches short so that it passes the batsman at chest height and forces him either to play a stroke at it or to take action to avoid it. Unless overused, it is a tactically legitimate weapon, for it surprises the batsman, or should do if it is not blatantly telegraphed, and unsettles him or hurries him into a shot which can be his downfall.

The great controversy over bouncers develops when one side has the bowlers fast enough, and good enough, to bowl them, so that the opposition is totally unsettled; and the opposition does not have the bowlers fast enough or good enough to reciprocate.

FIELDING

However good the bowler, however capable he is of bowling a bouncer or any other type of delivery, he will achieve nothing without the support of fielders and appropriate field-placing. A bouncer is not going to bowl a batsman out. If it takes his wicket, it is because it touches his glove on the way through to the wicket-keeper, or because he fends it off into the hands of short-leg, or because he attempts to hook it

Gower takes
evasive action at
silly point.

and skies it to square-leg or long-leg, and a field must be placed accordingly to accept the chance.

It is surprising how often a captain and a bowler signal their intentions by setting two long-legs or having two men on the square-leg boundary, yet the batsman still succumbs and pulls the bouncer straight into the hands of the waiting fielder.

Most captains will start a match with an attacking field, that is where fielders are placed in catching positions, positions which are obviously aimed at trying to get the batsman out rather than to stop him scoring runs. A defensive field is set only as a last resort, for it means that you have surrendered the initiative to the other side and your sole interest is to prevent them from scoring runs.

An attacking field will have fielders in 'silly' positions very close to the bat. When you have fielded at short-leg or at any bat-pad position you realise why such positions are called silly. The word means just what it implies – the silliness of exposing oneself to danger, especially when one is not even being paid to do so!

Terms such as silly mid-off and silly mid-on have long been in use, but the term bat-pad is comparatively new and has grown in use since fielders have moved closer to the wicket through the aids of helmets and padding. The object of such positions is to snap up catches which come when the batsman misreads the line or turn of the ball which comes off the edge of his bat and is deflected into his pads from which it rebounds. It is a further example of the changing vocabulary of cricket.

To watch men like Brian Hardie, David Gower and Mike Gatting fielding in bat-pad positions is exciting, but it is not a wise course for the club or village cricketer to follow. The English Schools Cricket Association has a ruling forbidding youngsters playing in games under their jurisdiction from fielding in silly positions. It is a wise ruling.

Few bowlers in first-class cricket can maintain the impeccable control of an Underwood, an Emburey or an Alderman. There is none at a lower level who can do so, particularly when the game is played on a doubtful wicket, and to field in a 'suicide' position, invariably without a helmet, in such circumstances would seem foolhardy in the extreme.

So the language of cricket grows. It is not a language that you have to sit down and learn; rather it is one that you will acquire over a period of time. Like all else in the game, a greater knowledge brings a deeper understanding, and you are the better for it.

A better understanding of the terms used in cricket will help when watching the game, and when listening to the comments of those who play it professionally and those who write and broadcast about it. Cricket is a game where much can be learned from watching the efforts of others, recognising their strengths and their weaknesses, and it is this aspect that will be dealt with in the next section.

6 LOOKING AT OTHERS

Any schoolmaster will tell you that if he has a couple of good cricketers in his team, the ability of the whole side will gradually improve. By watching the style and technique of the better players, moderate players develop their own game. They learn by imitation and improve accordingly.

In county cricket, there is a comradeship that is beneficial to everyone. Within a county side, players study each other's strengths and weaknesses and advise where they can. Your batting partner can be of tremendous help to you if things are going wrong in the middle. He can often tell you the mistakes you are making and suggest ways in which you can cope.

Ted Dexter recalled that in one of his first Test matches in Australia he hit Benaud for four and felt very pleased with himself, but he was a little taken aback when Colin Cowdrey, who was batting at the other end, beckoned to him to meet for a chat and then said, 'That's just what he wants you to do. If you play that shot again, you'll be out.' Advice is not always welcomed by the young, and a few moments later Dexter was caught behind when he tried to repeat the shot.

Young wicket-keeper Steve Marsh learned a tremendous amount by watching Alan Knott, and it was always apparent that whenever young keepers played against Kent they studied Knotty very closely and sought his advice.

On the county circuit players' strengths and weaknesses are debated, and you can be sure that if you are particularly vulnerable in any area, everyone will soon know about it. Even the greatest of players have weak spots.

If you are particularly vulnerable in any area, everyone will soon know about it and exploit it

WATCHING BATSMEN

There was a feeling that Clive Rice, early in an innings, was likely to clip a catch towards mid-on, and most sides placed a fielder in that position, closer than was customary for mid-on, but certainly not in a short or silly position. The West Indians set a silly mid-off for Chris Tavaré during his long innings against them in the Lord's Test of 1980. Chris had orders to stay at the wicket, and his top hand had come so far round in his desire to offer stubborn defence that the West Indians felt that he was always likely to give a bat-pad catch when he pushed forward defensively.

Bowlers will always discuss how they bowl to Ian Botham, Viv Richards or Graham Gooch, while batsmen inevitably talk about how Malcolm Marshall and Sylvester Clarke are bowling and what to expect next time they come up against them. Obviously, the same sort of discussions go on at club or village level. All of us now have the advantage of seeing so much cricket on television that we are able to study the methods of the world's greatest players, often with the benefit of long, lingering action replays. We can assess the strengths and even the flaws of the international stars, and if we are balanced in our judgement, note what we can do to enhance our own game and what we should leave alone because we do not possess the mark of genius.

Viv Richards is one of the best examples to cite. He is supremely confident in his own ability and when he was younger gave the impression that he believed he could score off every ball that was bowled to him. Unfortunately for those who played against him, but fortunately for those who paid to watch, he almost proved that he *could* score from every ball. Yet which of us could hope to emulate him?

He possesses two qualities that cannot be copied: he seems to have an uncanny knack of knowing just where the ball is going to pitch, and an equally uncanny ability to time the ball perfectly on the leg side for anything remotely pitched up or in line with the stumps. This results in him appearing to play across the line, fatal for most batsmen from the schoolboy upwards, but genius in Viv Richards, for he never misses. His timing is such that he always seems to hit the ball with great ferocity. His power is awesome.

One shot can be quoted as an example of the Richards genius, and it is one that can still be seen on the BBC video of the match in question. In 1979 England met West Indies in the Prudential World Cup Final at Lord's. West Indies had been in some trouble before Viv Richards and Collis King came together in a violent stand. Richards scored a century and hit Mike Hendrick for six on the last ball of the innings.

Hendrick was a relentlessly accurate medium-pace bowler who could move the ball appreciably. His final delivery in the West Indian innings was intended to be a yorker on off stump. For his part, Hendrick did everything right. The only problem was that Richards, with that spark of genius that can only be wondered at, anticipated the ball that was to be bowled, was outside the line of the off stump when it arrived, and hit it high into the Mound Stand for six. Now even if one accepts that a yorker on off stump was the most likely delivery to be bowled at that stage, Richards still had to adjust his position late enough for the bowler not to change his mind and then time the ball to such perfection that he hit it for six. Few other players would have dared to play the shot. Even fewer would have succeeded with it, and none should be advised to attempt it!

When watching Richards at a match or on television, particularly with the advantage of replays, we are able to analyse what he does, although it is not always easy to come up with an answer as to how to curb him when next you play against him. His liking for leg-side hitting would suggest that the slow

Opposite:
Power and majesty of the great artist. Richards drives imperiously through the off-side.

left-arm bowler might have some success against him early in an innings. He can offer chances at short-leg by the nature of the way in which he plays, but they are very few, and if you miss one you are not likely to be offered a second chance. Furthermore, not many sides set a short-leg fielder when he is batting.

Others have suggested that if you bowl to him just outside the off stump and make him stretch for his off-drive, his left foot is sometimes not to the pitch of the ball and therefore he is vulnerable, but he hits through the ball so hard that this can be a vain hope. It has been said that he relies so much on a good eye rather than a perfect technique that his powers must dim, but he has been playing Test cricket for fourteen years now and, as the West Indians recently discovered, his eye shows no sign of dimming yet.

In contrast, Sunil Gavaskar has decided to call it a day and he ended his international career in the **Sunil Gavaskar is the epitome of the batsman who plays straight** semi-final of the World Cup in India. He differs from Richards in every way and an aspiring batsman could find no better model. Gavaskar is the epitome of the batsman who plays straight. He shows the full face of the blade of the bat hanging down straight and, to the bowler, broad. There is an air of 'you shall not pass' about him, and he is a most difficult man to bowl at. The other great quality, and one which many envy, is his power of concentration. The bat is almost exclusively vertical, rarely horizontal, when Gavaskar is batting. He eschews risk and has the patience to build an innings. All that he does is founded on a sound technique. He is a different type of genius to Richards, but still a genius, and to watch him is to learn the correct art of batting.

Gordon Greenidge, Hampshire and West Indies, is another who is technically correct in his batting. He combines the qualities of both Richards and Gavaskar, yet a possible flaw springs from what is also one of his strengths. He is a violent striker of the ball and eager to hit from the start. He is technically sound and with his willingness to play shots can wrest the advantage away from you from the start of a match.

It is his eagerness to get on top of the bowling, however, which may also present a chance to get him out. If you watch him carefully, you will notice that sometimes a sense of frustration creeps in if he is subdued for any period of time. It is at this point that bowling accuracy can cause him to play a rash shot and surrender his wicket. It is almost as if he predetermines his shot before the ball is bowled, and this can be a vulnerability. However, it is not easy to discover flaws in great players such as Greenidge.

Gavaskar, full of concentration, purposeful and the broadest of straight bats.

Ian Botham is another batsman who does not enjoy it if the scoreboard is static. He has been accused of throwing his wicket away on occasions with misjudged hooks, pulls and sweeps, orthodox and reversed, but balance these errors against the number of runs he has scored in all types of cricket and the equation is very much in Ian's favour. Technically, he has been accused of having defensive weaknesses, particularly when playing forward to a good spin bowler, but his enormous power helps

Botham, a law unto himself, dismisses the ball from his presence.

him to surmount these flaws. He is so positive in his approach to batting that he is able to compensate for any technical deficiency. He may not quite get his left foot to the pitch of the ball, but he follows through so emphatically, straight and true, that he can still hit the ball out of the ground. The example of Ian Botham that one may follow is that once he has decided to play a shot, he plays it. There is no indecision in what Botham does, so that the ball is always likely to be travelling fast and hard when he hits it.

To watch him bat is an exciting experience and he is worth watching carefully to note the free flow of his shots and the positivity of all that he does. Another BBC video on which he is pictured is that which covers the remarkable Test series of 1981 between England and Australia. At Old Trafford, Botham reached a thrilling hundred and hit 66 in eight overs. He hooked Dennis Lillee, one of the greatest fast bowlers the world has known, for three incredible sixes. Two of them could be copied by nobody. They were more like overhead smashes at tennis, but they went for six because **The great example Ian Botham sets to** Botham went through with his shot and **everyone is to be positive in what you do** hit the ball hard. The great example Ian Botham sets to everyone is to be positive in what you do.

While we are talking of Ian Botham we must mention, too, his bowling, for it bears many of the characteristics of his batting. He has his off days, as we all do, when you notice that his run to the wicket is less purposeful than usual, but at his best he is a very difficult bowler to cope with. He will bowl several bad balls, but his strength is his infinite variety and, again, his positive approach. It has been said that he gets wickets with bad balls. This is probably true, and the reason is that you never know what is coming next. Next time you watch him, live or on television, study the six balls of an over carefully and you will see that no two balls are alike. He is never afraid to experiment. He is always attacking.

You can see his positive, aggressive approach to the game in his fielding, standing closer at slip than anyone else – but he holds some marvellous catches. One cannot hope to emulate his reactions; only a man so blessed could have taken the caught and bowled he took in the Edgbaston Test against Pakistan in 1987. We can all strive to copy his consistently positive, attacking approach to the game, but we must always remember the basics.

Mike Gatting is another whose approach is positive. Watch him as he comes to the wicket. He is swinging his arms, flailing his bat, and when he reaches the crease you know that he means business. It is almost as if he has wrested the advantage from the bowler before he has faced a ball. When he moves down the wicket the bowler can see only the stocky, powerful frame eager to hit the ball. There is no encouragement by a glimpse of the stumps: Gatting presents an almost impenetrable barrier. And no man displays better footwork in dealing with slow bowling.

You may notice an over-indulgence in the sweep which he executes effectively, but which it would not always be wise to copy, and there was a time when there was a hesitancy on the line of the off stump, but Gatting should be studied for the way he works at his game. When you hear words like resource and application, you need only look at Gatting to know what they mean.

In a different way, Graham Gooch dominates the bowlers. He always looks sleepy when he comes to the wicket, and he inevitably seems more concerned to hit boundaries than to run quick singles, but he is a powerful player like Ian Botham. He may not quite get to the pitch of the ball on occasions, but he goes through with his shots with a sort of awesome majesty.

WATCHING BOWLERS

Inevitably, we have become bogged down with batsmen, and it is time we looked at some bowlers. While batsmen have idiosyncracies of style which cannot be imitated, several of the top bowlers offer a model which all would do well to copy.

Mike Holding's beautifully smooth run to the wicket, with the athletic leap into the final delivery stride, is a fine example for any aspiring quick bowler. His action is high and this, allied to the powerful impetus he gets from the smoothness of his run-up, gives him his pace through the air. Although he has retired from Test cricket, he still performs splendidly for Derbyshire, and he has made them a particularly effective side in one-day cricket.

His place as the West Indies' leading fast bowler has passed to Malcolm Marshall, and there is a strong similarity between them. Again there is economy of style. Marshall, in run-up and high action, is in control of his body. There is never the feeling when you are watching him that his body is running away with

Opposite:
Malcolm Marshall.
High action and an
economy of style. A
bowler to watch as
a model and to
admire.

him, that he is tearing recklessly up to the wicket in order to generate pace. His speed comes from his rhythm, action and control, and he, like Holding, is one whose action could be emulated.

Outside the two West Indians there are two notable veterans who deserve the closest scrutiny whenever the opportunity presents itself: John Lever and Richard Hadlee.

John Lever, the Essex and England left-arm fast-medium swing bowler, has been at the top of his profession for nearly twenty years. When you watch him the first instinct is to believe that his run is unnecessarily long because he glides to the wicket at no great pace, yet his run gives him his rhythm which is the vital factor. Length of run is not necessary to produce speed. Many bowlers at junior level come racing towards the wicket only to stop and stutter in the final strides and, in effect, to gain whatever pace they do achieve only from the last couple of steps; the rest has been superfluous. Lever's pace and precision are achieved through rhythm.

As a left-arm bowler, he slants the ball across the batsman naturally, but he also swings the ball back into the right-handed batsman. His greatest strength is that he bowls straight. You have to play at every ball he bowls, and if you watch him in a limited-over game you will note that he pitches the ball well up into the block-hole so that he is constantly tucking the batsman up and fretting him.

With the advancing years, his arm is not quite as high as it used to be. You will see that this is because he drops his right shoulder a little, and if you watch carefully, you will be able to analyse the effect that this has on the delivery action.

In every way, however, John Lever is a model for any aspiring player. He has maintained a wonderfully high level of fitness, has never lost his enthusiasm for the game and is still the stiffest of opponents in the friendliest of manners.

The other veteran mentioned earlier is Richard Hadlee, now no longer of Nottinghamshire, but still very much New Zealand's leading bowler. He and Lever have the same dedication to fitness and have achieved a similar rhythm in their bowling.

Hadlee must rank as one of the greatest fast bowlers of all time, yet his run to the wicket is shorter than many club players who do not have a tenth of his pace. He has striven for economy of exertion so that the pace is in the high arm action and smoothness of approach. The magnificent thing to watch in his bowling is the subtlety of variation. To watch him is to see a thinking bowler. There are gradations of movement, adjustments of length and pace. He will probe for a batsman's weakness, but he will provide the killer blow only when it is sure to succeed. He swings the ball late, which makes him so difficult to play, and he is very serious in his study of and application to the game. Like Marshall and Holding, he is totally in control of his own body and knows exactly what he wants wrist, arm and shoulder to do at any one moment.

Among the slow bowlers, John Emburey's off-breaks are achieved with an excellent body action. His front foot lands in front of the middle and leg stumps so that, in fact, there are no bowlers in the game who bowl closer to the stumps than he does. For an off-break bowler it is essential to bowl close to the stumps, although some might suggest that Emburey is too unflagging in his adherence to this principle and could well vary his use of the crease more on occasions. What is most impressive about Emburey is his consistent rhythm. He gets into the groove and can go on bowling for hours, giving nothing away, with never a hint of encouragement for the batsman.

Watching on television or from the ring, it is not easy to appreciate how much he is spinning the ball, but what you should look for are his variations in flight and in the type of delivery he bowls. He uses the floater, but he also spears the ball in at the batsman, often tying him up around leg stump. A good exercise is to try to reason why he is bowling as he is. Do the conditions or the context of the match demand such

a type of bowling? Why has he set a particular field? It is also interesting to note why a bowler is bowling badly, if he is doing so. Emburey rarely bowls badly, but in his earlier days he tended to drop his arm slightly and so not use his full height to the advantage which it can give him. Compare his style with that of Eddie Hemmings, who tends to be more round-arm. This could be because Eddie turned to spin bowling at a mature age.

It is interesting to see which off-break bowlers give the ball more air. Vic Marks and Rodney Ontong tend to, although both adapt to one-day cricket where the former has been particularly successful. Emburey tends to bowl flatter and quicker in the one-day game, and he is extremely difficult to score from.

Phil Edmonds was an excellent slow left-arm bowler to study, although perhaps a little too experimental at times. He spun the ball a lot, had a high action and much variety. When position on the ground or television camera coverage allowed you to see straight down the wicket, it was possible to appreciate the loop that Edmonds got on the ball when he flighted it. The same applies to bowlers like John Childs, Rajesh Maru or Nick Cook. The loop that the ball makes in the air when they deliver it is an essential part of the armoury, and in studying it you can begin to understand the subtleties and the intelligent thinking of the spinner.

It is an art which is learned only after many years, and to study it is fascinating. It needs patience, constant hard work and self-belief.

WICKET-KEEPERS AND FIELDERS

Finally, a word should be said in this section about wicket-keepers and fielders. So much of the attention is on the batsman and the bowler, but a study of the best fielders in the game can be most rewarding.

Although his throwing arm is not what it was, David Gower is still a delight to watch. In the covers he always seems to be in time with the ball so that he can swoop on it and flick it back to the keeper in

Opposite:
Phil Edmonds, a high action and a willingness to flight the ball.

one movement. It is never running away from him. Note, too, the positioning of the slips. Botham alone adopts an unorthodox stance and placing, but ones suited to his abilities and reactions, while others are in a position of anticipation which can be copied to advantage.

The good fielder assumes that every ball is coming to him. What must be remembered is that you spend more time fielding than you do either batting or bowl-ing. A realisation of this fact is essential if you are to maintain the necessary concentration. When you survey a fielding side at a match or on television note how no one should need to be shouted at or clapped at by his captain or by the bowler. The good fielder remains alert to captain, bowler and what is happening all the time.

The good fielder assumes that every ball is coming to him

By the nature of events, all players will miss a catch once or twice a season, but this does not label a man a bad fielder. Alertness to what is going on is the basic requirement.

You can also note the different ways in which different fielders take a catch. The older, more conventional method was to hold the hands cupped, but fielders like Gooch have adopted the modern style of hands held in front of the face. Study both and adopt that which suits you. The important factor is to catch the ball.

Something else to look out for when watching a fielding side is that the task is being enjoyed. When you cease to enjoy fielding you are losing, conceding the advantage to the other side.

The hub of any fielding side is undoubtedly the wicket-keeper

The hub of any fielding side is the wicket-keeper. It is his example and vitality which keep the side on their toes in the field. Alan Knott was a tremendous inspiration, for he was such a magnificent keeper, likely to take an 'impossible' catch at any moment. His successor, Steve Marsh, is a great team man, ever encouraging and keeping lively throughout the longest, hottest day.

Keepers like Paul Downton, 'Jack' Russell of Gloucestershire and Bruce French are unhurried and

Opposite:
Wicket-keeper Paul Downton. Unhurried and unfussy and an inspiration to the fielders.

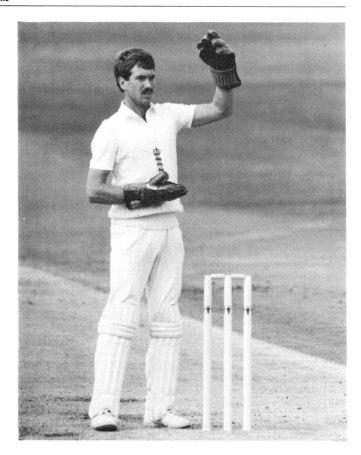

Bruce Fench, calm
and unruffled.

... and athletic
when necessary.

unfussy in all that they do. If you watch them carefully you will see that they are perfectly balanced, and their lack of histrionics is due to this fact. Other keepers, such as Jack Richards and David East, rely more on their athleticism. Once again it is a question of what your natural ability suits you to.

The purpose of this book is to encourage people to participate in cricket rather than to spend their time watching, but this section should have given some indication of the benefit that can be gained from watching cricket on television or elsewhere.

Even the best of players have faults, and it is helpful to the less experienced player to recognise this and to note how some who play the game professionally compensate for technical deficiencies. One should be encouraged to recognise that Botham, Gooch and Gower do not always get to the pitch of the ball when driving, but still manage to hit it for four. Perhaps that is their privilege!

7 FACTS AND FIGURES

The purpose of this final section is to lead you towards places and associations where you can find out more about the game and where you can gain all the information that you need in order to help you to play the game and learn about its structure.

The laws of the game are in the hands of the Marylebone Cricket Club, the famous MCC, and they can be contacted at the headquarters of the game:

The Secretary
MCC
Lord's Cricket Ground
St John's Wood
London NW8 8QN

The MCC also has an extensive museum and library and the Curator, Stephen Green, organises tours of the ground for parties. He, of course, can be contacted at the Lord's address.

Lord's is also the address of the National Cricket Association of which we have spoken a great deal already, and of the Test and County Cricket Board. The TCCB administers the first-class game in England including the four national competitions – the Britannic Assurance County Championship; the NatWest Bank Trophy; the Benson and Hedges Cup; the Refuge Assurance League – as well as the Cornhill Insurance Test matches and the Texaco Trophy one-day internationals.

The Britannic Assurance County Championship consists of three- and four-day matches which are played between the beginning of the season in April and the end of the season at the beginning of September. The NatWest Bank Trophy is the sixty-over knockout competition which begins on a Wednesday towards the end of June and reaches its climax with the final at Lord's on the first Saturday in September. The early rounds of the Benson and Hedges Cup are played in May and early June. They are played on a league basis of four divisions and each match is fifty-five overs per innings. The top two sides in each group pass into the quarter-finals and the tournament then becomes a knockout competition which has its final at Lord's on a Saturday towards the end of July. The fourth competition, the Refuge Assurance League, is a forty-over contest which is played on Sunday afternoons. As from 1988, the top four sides will decide the championship by playing semi-finals and a final in the second week in September.

Lord's is the home of the MCC, and it should be noted that although the MCC, the National Cricket Association and the TCCB share the same address at Lord's, they are separate bodies and each is responsible for a different province of the game.

Obviously, one of the best methods of finding out more about the game is to contact your local county club. Your county club is not concerned solely with selling membership of the club. It will give full details of indoor cricket schools, coaching facilities and other aids to cricketers that are available. Middlesex, Kent, Essex and Warwickshire are just four counties that have indoor schools, while big developments are taking place at The Oval and Northampton. Every county is now in a position to offer some sort of assistance to the aspiring cricketer of whatever standard. The addresses and telephone numbers of the county secretaries are as follows.

Derbyshire CCC
County Ground
Nottingham Road
Derby DE2 6DA (0332) 383211

Essex CCC
County Ground
New Writtle Street
Chelmsford CM2 0PG (0245) 354533

Glamorgan CCC
Sophia Gardens
Cardiff CF1 9XR (0222) 42478

Gloucestershire CCC
Phoenix County Ground
Nevil Road
Bristol BS7 9EJ (0272) 45216

Hampshire CCC
Northlands Road
Southampton SO9 2TY (0703) 333788

Kent CCC
St Lawrence Ground
Old Dover Road
Canterbury CT1 3NZ (0227) 456886

Lancashire CCC
County Cricket Ground
Old Trafford
Manchester M16 0PX (061) 848 7021

Leicestershire CCC
County Cricket Ground
Grace Road
Leicester LE2 8AD (0533) 831880

Middlesex CCC
Lord's Cricket Ground
London NW8 8QN (01) 289 1300

Northamptonshire CCC
County Ground
Wantage Road
Northampton NN1 4TJ (0604) 32917

Nottinghamshire CCC
Trent Bridge
Nottingham NG2 6AG (0602) 821525

Somerset CCC
The County Ground
St James's Street
Taunton TA1 1JT (0823) 72946

Surrey CCC
Kennington Oval
London SE11 5SS 01-582 6660

Sussex CCC
County Ground
Easton Road
Hove BN3 3AN (0273) 732161

Warwickshire CCC
Edgbaston
Birmingham B5 7QU (021) 440 4292

Worcestershire CCC
County Ground
New Road
Worcester WR2 4QQ (0905) 422694

Yorkshire CCC
Headingly Cricket Ground
Leeds LS6 3BU (0532) 787394

Outside the seventeen First-Class Counties, there are several other associations which will be of assistance. There are many Minor County clubs and they can be contacted through:

Minor Counties Cricket Association
Thorpe Cottage
Mill Common
Ridlington
North Walsham NR28 9TY

Cricket is very popular in both Scotland and Ireland, and information can be gained from:

Scottish Cricket Union
18 Ainslie Place
Edinburgh EH3 6AU

Irish Cricket Union
45 Foxrock Park
Foxrock
Dublin 18
Eire

Two other addresses are of vital importance for anyone who is looking for help and guidance. The first is for women. The Women's Cricket Association operates from:

16 Upper Woburn Place
London WC1 0QP

The body that was founded in order to encourage sport throughout the country and to make sport possible for all is:

Border cuts, Athey leaps for safety, and French's eyes never leave the ball.

The Sports Council
16 Upper Woburn Place
London WC1 0QP

Again, the same address as the WCA, but a separate body.

There are two cricket magazines published each month which not only give news and information regarding all aspects of the game, but carry many advertisements related to equipment for sale and to clubs who are on the lookout for players.

They are *The Cricketer International,* which has been in operation since 1921, and *Wisden Cricket Monthly,* which was first published in 1979. They each cost £1.10, but they are available from the reading rooms of most libraries. They will be beneficial in leading you towards good equipment at reasonable prices and in helping you to make contact with like-minded people.

The game itself is very well documented. If you want to learn all about the first-class game throughout the world, the two best annuals are:

Benson and Hedges Cricket Year, edited by David Lemmon, published by Pelham Books, which is profusely illustrated. It is published each November and deals with the cricket year recently finished.

Wisden Cricketers' Almanack, edited by Graeme Wright, published by John Wisden. This covers the same period as the other annual, but is issued in April of the following year.

Both are fine reference books, but both are expensive, and they can first be referred to at your local library.

At £1.75 **Playfair Cricket Annual**, edited by Bill Frindall, published each April and sponsored by NatWest Bank, is excellent value. It is a paperback pocket book with details of all county players and results of Test matches etc.

These three books, of course, are mostly concerned with first-class cricket. School, club and village cricket is less well documented. The best coaching manuals available were mentioned in an earlier section, and as they vary in standard, it should be emphasized that the best available coaching or instructional books are those issued by the officers of or under the guidance of the NCA and the TCCB. Their concern is to foster the game, and they are the work of experts.

Videos have become increasingly popular and increase in number week by week. They are expensive to buy, but easy to borrow for a small fee from most libraries.

John Gaustad
Sportspages
Cambridge Circus Shopping Centre
Charing Cross Road
London WC2H 0JG   **(01–240 9604)**

can give all information on the cricket videos available, but it should be pointed out that this is a commercial concern and that he sells books and videos for his living.

One last list of those who are eager to help and encourage lovers of cricket of all ages is that of cricket societies.

There are cricket societies in various parts of England and Scotland – Blackley, Chesterfield, The Cricket Society (London), The Cricket Society (Midlands), The Cricket Society (West

of England), East Riding, Essex, Fylde, Hampshire, Cleckheaton, Lancashire and Cheshire, Lincolnshire, Merseyside, Leeds, Nottingham, Rotherham, Glasgow and Edinburgh, Somerset, Cardiff, Stourbridge, Sussex, West Lancashire, Wombwell, and Oxford and Cambridge Universities. They have regular meetings at which noted speakers talk about the game, and they assist young players by means of coaching courses, scholarships and colts tours. The address of your nearest society can be obtained from:

The Secretary
The Council of Cricket Societies
205 Hyde Park Road
Leeds
Yorkshire L56 1AH

All these addresses and people whom you can contact, all the books and the videos and the details of famous players, should be seen only as a supplement to participating in the game yourself. In the end, none of the reading, nor the videos, nor the discussion can be a substitute for playing the game. That is where the real enjoyment lies. There are no boundaries of ability. Enthusiasm, endeavour and love of the game are all that are required. As John Arlott, one of the most famous and best-loved of cricket commentators, once said: 'All cricketers are cricketers, none the less so for not being "first-class", which is no more than a statistical distinction.'